POET'S ENGLAND 11

LEICESTERSHIRE AND RUTLAND

Compiled by Guy Stapleton

Illustrated by Gillian Durrant

Brentham Press

First published 1992 by
Brentham Press, 40 Oswald Road, St Albans, Herts AL1 3AQ.

ISBN 0 905772 33 4

British Library Cataloguing-in-Publication Data.
A catalogue record for this book is available from the British Library.

DTP by Northern Writers Advisory Services, Sale, Cheshire M33 4DN.
Printed in England by Kerrypress Ltd, Luton, Beds.

FOREWORD

Leicestershire and Rutland are in 'The Shires', that expression redolent of rolling pastures punctuated by people on horseback. It is right still to think of these counties in the plural because, although Rutland may be for formal purposes a part of Leicestershire, it has done more than any other county since the much-lamented local government reorganisation of 1974 to keep its separate industry and character.

On a map they form an irregular parallelogram in the centre of England, with Rutland occupying a rough triangle in the bottom right-hand corner. Leicestershire is divided by the River Soar into the industrial villages of the west, with the craggy mass of Charnwood Forest in its midst, and the Wolds to the east, the country of beautiful meadows and green fields, gentle hills and woods so much admired by William Cobbett. Rutland gradually declines eastwards into the Lincolnshire lowlands, its swells being interspersed by valleys such as the rich Vale of Catmose and by the largest man-made lake in Europe, Rutland Water. After agriculture and mining, the staple industries are hosiery and shoemaking.

Much of the verse about these counties has been as gentle as its landscape. Appropriately, the earliest item in this collection is Thomas Tusser's 1573 description of its champaign country. Thereafter the poetry of Leicestershire and Rutland moved from the 17th century versified travel journals of Richard Corbet and John Taylor, Michael Drayton's more substantial Poly-Olbion, and more delicate lyrics of Thomas Bancroft, John and Francis Beaumont, to the panegyrics of such 18th century poets as J. Duick, W. P. Taylor and William Woty. The 19th century brought major figures such as William Wordsworth, John Clare and Thomas Moore, as well as people as varied as Fanny Kemble, the actress, Edward Thring, headmaster of Uppingham, and the 5th Duke of Rutland; and a wealth of hunting songs and folk ballads whose length and ephemeral references unfortunately preclude their inclusion here. The 20th century has seen more personal reactions to the beauties and changes in the two counties, and what has heartened me immensely in making this selection is the amount and vigour of poetry of this kind being written there today. I have drawn not only on authors such as the TV and radio personality Mike Read, but on a number of previously unpublished poets in making this word-tapestry of two counties across four centuries.

January 1992   *Guy Stapleton*

iii

ACKNOWLEDGMENTS

For the use of copyright material acknowledgment is made to the following:
The estate of Judith Bickle and Robert Hale Ltd. for 'Market Harborough' from *This is My Harvest* (1955). The Poetry Society for 'Rutland' by John Bull from *Poetry Review*, 76, 1/2 (1986). The estate of Leonard Clark for 'Great Casterton' from *English Morning and Other Poems* (Hutchinson, 1953). The author and J.M. Dent & Sons Ltd. for 'Derbyshire Born, Monmouth is my Home' by Clifford Dyment from *Experiences and Places* (1955). The author and *Punch* for 'Miners' Leicestershire' by Edgar Pole (published in *Punch*, 6 June 1951). The author for 'Rutland' by Mike Read from *Elizabethan Dragonflies* (Goodyer Associates, 1988). Leicester Poetry Society for 'Footpath to Lyddington' by Barry Roberts from *Lines from Leicester* (1988).

Every effort has been made to trace copyright holders and any omissions will be rectified if notified. For previously unpublished poems the copyright remains with the authors. Poems are dated from the first year of publication, where this is known.

LEICESTERSHIRE & RUTLAND: Map showing main place names mentioned in the text.

CONTENTS

LEICESTERSHIRE

LEICESTERSHIRE

from
LEICESTERSHIRE

Whilst other writers, in harmonious verse,
Of various climes the various charms rehearse;
Climes which they partially exalt to fame –
Let none an inoffensive scribbler blame,
If he of his attempts the worth to raise,
And of Leicestria's land to speak the praise.

Say then, Sylvanus, shall we first recite
What's its utility, or what delight?
Or shall we rather the transactions note
Of days of old, and ancient records quote?

Each in its turn: can any spot of ground,
Tho' we search Albion through, more rich be found,
Than what Leicestria's fertile realms afford,
With cattle, corn, and herbage, amply stor'd?

Twere most ungenerous here, and most unfit,
Thy commendation, Bakewell, to omit,
Whose judgement, skill, and well-digested thought,
Our cattle's breed have to perfection brought.

Had Dyer at this later period liv'd,
What praises had our ample fleece receiv'd!
Whose worth let Halifax and Leeds proclaim;
And love the country whence the treasure came.

Ye sons of Nimrod, eager for the sport,
Here to your aged master pay your court;
The science of the Chace, by Meynell taught,
Its pleasures here enjoy, with health unbought.

*

Near Bosworth town, but not in Bosworth's field,
Richard, his crown and life compell'd to yield,

Discover'd, when too late, that power supreme
Was a mere shew, and pomp an empty dream!
No more thy bloody purpose, Murderer, seek,
For Murder, tho' it hath no tongue, will speak
"With most mirac'lous organ," – ever shun
Th' accursed deed, nor on thy ruin run!

Boast, Thurcaston, that thou to one gav'st birth
Than whom few better ever liv'd on earth;
The venerable Latimer, a name
Justly recorded in the book of fame;
The suff'ring Martyr in that glorious cause
Which gain'd the great reward – his God's applause.
From thee, Gracedieu, dramatic Beaumont came,
Temp'ring with cooler judgment Fletcher's flame.

Ye sons of Pride, ye creatures of a day,
Lo! Leicester's abbey, mouldring to decay!
Here rest the bones of Wolsey, – mark his fate;
The end of proud Ambition contemplate....
His virtues no memorial ask from me,
Shakespeare has penn'd his lasting eulogy.

1798   *W.P.Taylor*

LEICESTERSHIRE

In Leicestershire they hunt the fox
As other folk hunt gold.
A man without a hunting-box,
Or dressed in anything but pink,
Is not a man whom one would think
Of knowing; and I'm told
The merest babies' google-goos
Approximate to view-halloos.

In Leicestershire they dread the frost
As other folk dread pain;
In fact they're absolutely lost
When Jack congeals their darling earth;
The fox alone shows signs of mirth,
And, till it thaws again,
The huntsmen sit and smoke and sigh
Or eat another Melton pie.

1926   *E.V.Lucas*

8

CHAMPION COUNTRIE

There swineherd that keepeth the hog,
there neatherd, with cur and his horne,
There shepherd with whistle and dog,
be fence to the medowe and corne.
There horse being tide on a balke,
is readie with theefe for to walke.

Where all thing in common doth rest,
corne field with the pasture and meade,
Though common ye doo for the best,
yet what doth it stand ye in steade?
There common as commoners use,
for otherwise shalt thou not chuse.

What laier much better then there,
or cheaper (thereon to doo well?)
What drudgerie more any where
lesse good thereof where can ye tell?
What gotten by Sommer is seene:
in Winter is eaten up cleene.

Example by Leicestershire,
what soile can be better than that?
For any thing hart can desire,
and yet doth it want ye see what.
Mast, covert, close pasture, and wood,
and other things needfull as good.

1573   *Thomas Tusser*

PLACE RHYMES

Higham on the Hill,
Stoke in the Vale,
Wykin for buttermilk,
Hinckley for ale.

Sutton for mutton,
Bosworth for beef;
Carlton the pretty boy,
Coton the thief.

Bread for Borough men;
At Great Glenn
There are more great dogs than honest men.

9

from
DERBYSHIRE BORN, MONMOUTH IS MY HOME

Derbyshire born, Monmouth is my home,
Monmouth I call Wales despite cartographers,
My home for a few young years and now,
In spite of Leicestershire that schooled and fought me
And fights me still insisting in my blood.
Yes, Leicester got into my blood and made my bone –
Leicestershire loved me, its stubborn son
Who hated the no man's land, the elbower-out
of northern and southern culture, possesing none,
I declared in my youthful arrogance:
I saw the cinder paths of mining villages –
Ibstock, Moira, Ellistown –
The chip shop and the corner shop that sold
Racing tips and shameful novelettes;
I saw the dirty pub that loved the colliery
Like its fat and dirtier purse;
And I saw the migrations of miners moving
Across the coalfields from shift to shift
In the red Midlands buses they called Red Emmas,
Men's faces black, with rubber-dinghy lips
And floating eyes like nightmare nigger minstrels –
And as I saw I shuddered and cycled on,
Homeless and sick in the towns my home;
Cycled to Charnwood for its hobo roads,
Pre-Cambrian rocks and lonely lapwings,
Rock rose and oak and prairies of fern –
Cycled in solitude to meet a monk
Who stared from a long way off and did not speak.
Charnwood to me was a shape of fear:
Square Teutons of granite, blue jowls
Of bullying slate: I shuddered and ran
To the railway wagons with their owners' names
Painted along their sides like Yankee athletes',
And I was homeless again in Leicestershire.

But Leicester is in my eyes and mind: the Trappist
Tall in the mist, the crags like fangs,
The ruined abbeys, the smell of coal

Have mined in me like secret workings. Monmouth
I choose, but Leicestershire has chosen,
And lucky I am, reluctant, having a home
To-day when the world is homeless.

1955   *Clifford Dyment*

from
BRAVO! LEICESTERSHIRE!
(Leicestershire v The Australians, 3/4 July 1888)

Ye bold champion players, ye Mary'bone swells,
Whose prowess the cricketing chronicler tells,
Whom bright stars of the premier counties we call,
As ye flourish the willow or trundle the ball;
Stand around just for once – it's but fair "tit for tat" –
And, with Hornby excepted, each take off his hat
To the players who hail from those pastures so green,
Where in winter brave squadrons of scarlet are seen,
When their confines are blithe with the notes of the horn,
And alive with the flyers of Belvoir and Quorn.
You may laugh at our crowing – I care not a rap;
We've for once a brave feather to wear in our cap.
And I think, on the whole, it's by far the best plan,
As we've not many chances, to crow while we can.

Chorus
So right bravely you'll cheer while the story is told
How we lowered th'Australian banner of gold,
How the Leicestershire men nailed their flag to the mast,
Like the tars of Old England in days of the past,
And, in spite of their foemen's prestige on the green,
Got the best of the fight, though the struggle was keen.

1888   *Property Short*

11

MINERS' LEICESTERSHIRE

Derelict, idle, the rotting headstock,
The rusty, rackety, six-man cage
And the crumbling, tunnelless, lifeless smokestack
Speak of a bygone age.

Here where the springing thicket's thinning
Breaks on a granite-strewn, pock-marked mound
Lies the dearth of a still more ancient winning
Under the tired ground.

Tallow-dip, Sabbath-sun beasts of burden
Nor to return nor turn again,
But the sons of their sons who inherit the guerdon,
Miners – belatedly *men*!

    (Shades of old *Califat*, *California*,
    Ibstock, *Sinope*, bankless *Clink*,
    Number-Three, *Newbold* and flood-bound *Cutter*,
    Bug-and-Wink.)

A mile a minute the double-deck cages
Drumming the guides on the turning shift
Or the purr of the belt as the coal emerges
Out of the upcast drift.

Deeper and farther, the shaft and the coalface,
New risks rise from the perils of the past –
Is the Joy-loader jammed? There's a voice from the surface –
Call from the Hall – "Full mast!"

Lamped and helmeted, steel-shod, machine-aged,
Pick-and-shovel sinewed, schooled to the pen,
From the old pit-born to the rawest of the teen-aged,
Miners – *undoubtedly* men!

    (Modern miners of *Merryless*, *Nailstone*,
    Bagworth, *Ellistown*, *Leicester South*,
    Desford, *Whitwick* and older *Snibston*,
    and *New Lount*.)

1951　　　　　　　　　　　　　　　　*Edgar Pole*

MARKET HARBOROUGH

Came youthful April – so it was that when
Laburnum trees hung valances of gold
We sought the wide, delicious little street
Where "Angel," "Peacock," and the "Three Swans" meet;
And in one building seventeenth-century old
The Grammar School and Butter Market hold
Sweet secrets that they never may repeat:
There is a yardless church, and o'er these inns
A modern comfort spreads on ancient scene;
The flowery fields and contemplative kine
In one deep unity of peace combine:
An English country view in there beyond
Where drifts the polished grass spear, darkly green,
And wind-brushed poppies with the wheatears lean
Where now the April breeze ruffles the cloud
Of trefoil, and the thorny hedge is bowed
To blossoming may, its perfume swift and keen
Slashes our senses from each vale and dene.
In Leicestershire the hunt in form and mind
Leaps to the eye instinctively to please –
Until the tragic kill is heard and seen –
But there no so-called sport of death, unkind,
Can shake the lark's proud trill above the land
Nor move the wise trees that so firmly stand
About that wide, delicious little street
Where "Angel," "Peacock," and the "Three Swans" meet.

1947   *Judith Bickle*

13

from
CHURCH-LANGTON

On yonder broad circumference of ground,
Where chilling clay diffus'd its damp around,
Within whose bounds no luring charm was seen,
No tree to shelter, and no bush to screen.
The rich Plantation* now salutes our eyes,
And waves its foliage of enchanting dyes.
Through these inviting walks how sweet to rove!
Where shade to shade, and grove succeeds to grove,
Distinct, yet mixt, that at one view we see
Consistence heighten'd by variety.
These witching walks, sequester'd from the throng,
And hum of men, how sweet to muse along.

               *

Nor less attractive does the prospect stand,
When blust'ring winter howls throughout the land.
Then to the valley's bottom I descend,
The air's vast concave hear the tempest rend,
(Myself embower'd below, serene, and warm
In closest shelter,) and defy the storm,
Look up, and there my eye with wonder sees,
Due-rang'd, a waving theatre of trees.
Oaks, Pines, and Cedars, rattle at the blast,
And ev'ry motion seems to be the last.
This, this is dignity. Blow on, ye winds!
Blow on! and rouse our inattentive minds,
More than the calm soft-issuing from the sky,
The roaring tempest lifts the soul on high.

1770   *William Woty*

* Gumley Plantation

THE OLD DUNMORE TUNE
(Hallaton)

Old Dunmore's dead, that good old man,
Him we shall no more see.
He made these chimes to play themselves
At twelve, nine, six and three.

                         Anon.

14

FOSTON
Lost Village, Leicestershire

There is a field I know
Where sunshine on a winter's day
Can dazzle as in spring
Where lapwings circle
Over ploughed up soil
Their peewit wailings
Matching the moment.

There is a field I know
Where once an ancient village stood
Now ridged and furrowed
Turfed, moss overgrown
Boulders, stones
And unseen relics

Houses stood here
Peopled with problems
Death has erased the past
Now there are wailings and silence.

1992   *Anne Kind*

THEDDINGWORTH
Inscription on almsbox

If aught thou hast to give or lend,
This ancient British church befriend;
If poor but still in spirit willing,
Out with thy purse and give a shilling;
But if its depths should be profound,
Out with thy purse and give a pound.
Look for no record to be given
But trust to thy reward in Heaven.

Anon.

ODSTONE

Odstone of all places most odd,
With ne'er a beer-house nor yet a house of God;
On the top of a hill, not in a hole,
Neither good for your body nor good for your soul.

Trad.

from
THE HINCKLEY WHITSUNTIDE PROCESSION, 1792

Observe the Millers in their floury dress
And pageantry, their honours to express;
While we extol, by soft enchantment draws,
The whole assembly well deserves applause.

*

Next unto this, to hail the Cavalcade,
The Frame-Work Knitters to display their trade,
In martial pride and grandeur now appear,
And join in splendid manner, front and rear.

With Butchers, Joiners, and Cordwainers too,
In fancy dresses, pleasing to the view;
And other different trades, as we descry,
Striving each other to outvie.

1792   *Anon.*

16

LUTTERWORTH
(from Iter Boreale)

Our next Day's Stage was Lutterworth, a Town
Not willing to be noted, or set down
By any Traveller; for when we had been
Thro' at both Ends, we could not find an Inn;
Yet for the Church sake turn and light we must,
Hoping to find one Dram of Wickliff's Dust;
But we found none, for underneath the Pole,
No more rests of his Body, than his Soul:
Abused Martyr, how hast thou been torn
By two wild Factions! first the Papists burn
Thy Bones for Hate, the Puritans for Zeal
Do sell thy Marble, and thy Brass they steal.
A Parson met us there, who had great store
Of Livings, some say, but of Manners more:
In whose streight cheerful Age a Man might see
Well-govern'd Fortune, Bounty, Wife and Free.

1647   *Richard Corbet*

BOSWORTH
(from Song of the Plow)

Bring rue and hyssop to asperge
The chantry-tomb of bygone years!
Unto my song, become a dirge,
O Fount of Pity, lend thy tears:
King Richard's fall at Bosworth rang
A people's death, to wakeful ears.

1916   *Maurice Hewlett*

THE CLOSING OF THE MINES
(Bagworth Colliery, 9 February 1991)

The closing of the mines has now come around,
It's strange not to hear in my home town,
The noise of the plant so brightly lit,
All centred round the colliery tip.

In my boyhood days my playground to be
And in later years it was work for me;
The memories I have of those bygone years,
I still talk about over one or two beers.

Friendships were forged in those deep dark holes,
Where men had to work like human moles,
George, Albert, Roy and Ray,
All helped me through my hardworking day.

The noise of the pick and the shotfirer's boom,
Blasting away to make more room,
Black diamond they called it in its glory day,
With the passing of time now all gone away.

The damage it did to the place I was born
Moved families away feeling all forlorn,
The faces of men all wrinkled with time,
With visible signs of their work down the mine.

But they can't take away those memories I'll keep,
We still have a laugh whenever we meet,
I'll take with me to my dying day,
The making of friends along the way.

The pit has now gone but the people are still there,
And with all of them I know I can share
The rest of my time as the world goes around,
And the memories I have of my work underground.

1992   *J. Measom*

GRACEDIEU

Grace Dieu, that under Charnwood standst alone,
As a grande relicke of Religion,
I reverence thine old but fruitful worth,
That lately brought such noble Beaumonts forth,
Whose brave heroic muses must aspire
To match the anthems of the heavenly quire,
The mountains crowned with rocky fortresses,
And sheltering woods, secure thy happiness,
That highly favoured art (though lowly placed)
Of Heaven and with free Nature's bounty graced,
Herein grow happier, and that bliss of thine
Nor Pride o'ertop nor Envy undermine.

1639   *Thomas Bancroft*

IN A GARDEN OF COLEORTON
the Seat of Sir George Beaumont, Bart., Leicestershire

Oft is the medal faithful to its trust
When temples, columns, towers are laid in dust;
And 'tis a common ordinance of fate
That things obscure and small outlive the great:
Hence, when yon mansion and the flowery trim
Of this fair garden, and its alleys dim,
And all its stately trees are passed away,
This little niche, unconscious of decay,
Perchance may still survive. – And be it known
That it was scooped within the living stone, –
Not by the sluggish and ungrateful pains
Of labourer plodding for his daily gains;
But by an industry that wrought in love,
With help from female hands, that proudly strove
To aid the work, what time these walks and bowers
Were shaped to cheer dark winter's lonely hours.

1807   *William Wordsworth*

19

THE TALE OF THE MOIRA PIG

When Moira folk held a parade
'Twas a memorable event
Because of a decision made
By a local resident.

While "in his cups", so folk recall,
Though no-one knows just why,
That merry gent put th'pig on th'wall
To watch the band go by.

When everybody laughed he thought,
"This is a good idea.
It's such a joke I think I ought
To do it every year."

Then every year the puzzled swine
Was hoisted in position,
So th'pig on th'wall became, in time,
An old Moira tradition.

1992   *Ruby N. Ramsell*

ASHBY DE LA ZOUCH

They built a smashing castle here
beside an old ash tree.
The Zouch's came to live in it
from France across the sea.
But Oliver Cromwell caused a war
to cast away the crown,
so after Roundhead men laid siege
they knocked the castle down.
                    Ashby's changed, m'duck!

When Turpin robbed on Alton Hill
with trusty steed, Black Bess,
then crowds of villains filled our pubs –
a drunken mob, alas!
Yet when they built the Ashby Spa
some elegance was certain.
The gentry came with carriage and pair,
and the tramway went to Burton.
                    Ashby's much changed, m'duck!

The railway came from Leicester
in eighteen forty-nine
'til nineteen hundred and sixty-four
when Beeching closed the line.
Meanwhile the Spa had come and gone
and Ashby lost its fame
but Scott had written "*Ivanhoe*"
which brightens up the name.
                    Still Ashby's changing, m'duck!

The population grew and grew
some brand new shops were mooted.
Holdron's now sells drugs and skirts
and Ison's Smithed and Booted.
Circle Garage got knocked down
a supermarket flourished.
With Mews and Courtyards blossoming
the shoppers were well nourished.
                    Ashby really has changed, m'duck!

They've set two mini-roundabouts
at the end of Market Street.
The drivers seem to like 'em
they say it works a treat.
But pity the poor pedestrian
who only wants to shop
'cos the way across the junction now
is a quick jump, skip and hop.
                              Ashby's still changing, m'duck!

1992   *H.M. Chandler*

BREEDON CHURCH

Secure on your hilltop
Since time immemorial,
Serious windows,
Square solemn stones.
A no-nonsense tower,
And prim, private box-pews;
You stand with the broad yews,
Aloof, and alone,
Immune to the blasting,
The scraping and digging;
Un-moved by the men
Who are picking the bones
Of your insecure hilltop,
For gravel and stone.
Diminishing, vanishing,
Sinecure hilltop –
In time a memorial
Stone, on its own,
Will show where your tower,
And other such nonsense,
Stood solemn, and silent –
A fool? All alone?

1992   *Helen Brett*

22

from
IN GRANDAD'S DAY

We children hunted with the Quorn
If not too far away to hack
Our ponies to the meet – and back;
And, if it was a cubbing morn,
We rose at dawn with many a yawn
And off we got to Breedon Cloud
To slap our saddle flaps full loud
To keep the cubs in covers drawn.
We saw the golden sun arise
O'er Donington and stood around
The Ramsley Wood when deer were found.
... And when the days
For proper hunting came, we rode
For miles "at walk" or "trot" by road
And fields and tracks and bridle ways
And over stiles and timber rails,
(And yet not let our ponies sweat),
To get to meets in time, and set
About the walls and rocky dales
Of Charnwood. At half-past three we said
"Good night!" and let the girths go slack;
We had to hack our ponies back
Before the daylight went, and fed,
And brushed, and bedded down, and all
The dirty tack well dunked and hung
Before the bath time bell was rung
And supper served at Breedon Hall.
And as we dined we told our tales
Of daring deeds and frightful falls
And how we leapt those fearsome walls
And cantered up those verdant vales.
I dreamt, those nights, of runs that day,
Of ghostly hunts with phantom packs
From Hangman Stone to Battle Flats,
From Charnwood Heath to Stewards Hay,
From Whitwick Waste to Maple Well,
And Abbot's Oak to Agar's Nook,
To Swanimote and Becon Brook,

From Peldor Tor on past the shell
Of Ulverscroft's old Abbey Church
To Hammercliff and Breakback Hill,
And up Earls Dyke to Charley Mill,
To Chitterman and cross to search
In Craven's Rough. They gave their best
Up Beacon Hill then down the gorse
To Hanging Stones and right on course
To end the day at Black-Bird's Nest.

1992   *Gillies Shields*

from
EPISTLE TO THE LADY CHARLOTTE RAWDON
(Castle Donington)

Yet oh! believe me in this blooming maze
Of lovely nature, where the fancy strays
From charm to charm, where every floweret's hue
Hath something strange, and every leaf is new!
I never feel a bliss so pure and still,
So heavenly calm, as when a stream or hill,
Or veteran oak, like those remembered well,
Or breeze or echo, or some wild flower's smell
(For, who can say what small and fairy ties
The memory flings o'er pleasure as it flies?)
Reminds my heart of many a sylvan dream
I once indulged by Trent's inspiring stream;
Of all my sunny morns and moonlight nights
On Donington's green lawns and breezy heights!

1806   *Thomas Moore*

24

KEGWORTH

A beauteous village nestling by the Soar,
Where I've spent happy days in times of yore,
Near to "Moore's Walk"*, as now the people tell,
The Irish Bard would weave the mystic spell.
Where Kingston stands upon the emerald lea,
And Wymeswold church you in the distance see;
Good Lockington uprears her sacred fane,
Whose marble walls sweet memories retain.
Near Sawley, with her bridge across the Trent,
Where, with glad heart, my youthful steps I bent,
To seize the cowslip and the primrose sweet;
Returning by the spot where rivers meet,
Two sisters, Soar and Trent, in love unite:
No fairer scene bewitched by water sprite.
Sweet Kegworth! thou art dear unto my heart;
I'll not forget thee till with life I part.
I've watched the sunsets in the distant west,
As over Donington he sank to rest:
That village fair, near the enchanting park,
Sacred to flowers and sunshine, lay of lark;
Where dwell the heirs of that illustrious race,
Who to old England gave such worth and grace;
Now Kegworth, queen of rural scenes, farewell!
May abler bards thy many beauties tell,
But none shall love thee more, or long to be
Within thy precincts, 'neath my favourite tree;
A boon I ask, one blessing humbly crave,
That here my ashes find their final grave.

1902   *John Dainty*

* Thomas Moore, the celebrated Irish poet, lived some time here, and the villagers still show
his favourite walk.

25

HATHERN
Inscription for the Ruin of a Village Cross

The simple folk once used to throng
These mouldering steps beneath,
And every child that passed along
Its soft petitions breathe,
                    In pious days of yore.

The working-men at dawn of day
Were here assembled kneeling,
And to their labour bore away
A calm of holy feeling
                    In Christian days of yore.

Till once a stalwart company
Of men with gloomy faces,
Unlike the men ye used to see
In such-like holy places
                    In quiet days of yore,

With savage hands pulled down the sign
Of our Redeemer's sorrow,
And promised in more force to join,
And break the rest to-morrow, –
                    Hating the days of yore.

But Providence from then till now
This remnant hath befriended,
And by this shaft and time-worn steps
The memory hath defended
                    Of the good days of yore.

And still, whene'er the good and great
On common times pass nigh me,
Though no petition they repeat,
Nor kneel in silence by me,
                    As in the days of yore;

Yet blessed thoughts upon their hearths
From Heaven come gently stealing,
And each from his gray ruin parts
With calmer, holier feeling,
                    Blessing the days of yore.

1852   *Henry Alford*

from
LOUGHBOROUGH, AN ODE

Dear native town, tho' far remov'd
From thee and relatives belov'd,
Yet fancy's magick pow'r
Paints all thy pleasing scenes so true,
Thy shades, thy hills, thy meads I view,
And gently-winding Soar.

O hear me while th'Icarian star,
With sultry vapours taints the air,
To its cool silver streams:
There under bending osiers laid,
Let Phoebus and the Muses aid
My soft poetick dreams.

How dull the city views appear,
Where clouds of smoke pollute the air,
And dim the azure skies:
Her gilded spires, her num'rous piles,
Tho' stretch'd thro' sev'n extended miles,
Are scarce perceiv'd to rise.

The concourse of promiscuous throngs,
The clamour of discording tongues,
The ear with torture wound:
The rattling coaches constant din
Roars like a deluge in,
Or thunder's hoarser sound.

How welcome in exchange for these,
The zephyrs whisp'ring thro' the trees
The birds melodious trills:
The low of kine, the bleat of flocks,
The echoes from repeating rocks,
And sound of bubbling rills.

Such are the scenes which Loughbro' grace,
Such Garrenton, delightful place!
Haunts pleasing to the Muse:
Here wou'd the fates my wish befriend,
With a well-chosen book or friend,
To pass my hours I'd choose.

1735   *J. Duick*

IN LOUGHBOROUGH

in Loughborough
where the people
walk into you

where the bus
from Nottingham
is antique-gold and blue
and a girl
on the bus
puts on white
gloves
and we watch
enthralled
each every finger

approaching
the town
the landscape
is lit by
farmers
in curious lines
of orange fire
is lit with
seagulls
magnetised
to tiny tractors
and
here is the brook
of Brookside
and here is the
Bingo poster
still upside down
in Loughborough
where the people
walk into you

the salt sea
breeze
the Italians in
Mario's
the sun-lit
market
where people
walk into you

the songs by bells
the girls
playing rounders
this mad
inland
Blackpool
every shop
selling postcards

we'll get the bus
at 5 past 4
to converge with
the industrial
bicycles
home from Loughborough
where the people
walk into you.

1986   *Mark Stevenson*

ODE TO FLOBBS*

Old Flobbs is oft remembered
With his rugged, weathered face;
The grand old tramp of Loughborough
Who paced the Market Place.

He was always meek and gentle
And never did he frown;
His "pub" – the Fearon Fountain
In the heart of Loughborough Town.

Market traders gave him handouts;
He knew them by their names;
His "bedroom" – a draughty doorway
Outside Simpkin and James.

'Tis remembered when the Market Place
Seemed so forlorn one day;
The traders talked in whispers,
Dear old Flobbs had passed away.

1992   *Edward Mansell Buxton*

* William Smith, lovingly called Old Flobbs, was a tramp in Loughborough in the 1920s.

CHARNWOOD FOREST
(Poly-Olbion, Song XXVI)

O Charnwood, be thou cald the choycest of thy kind,
The like in any place, what Flood hath hapt to find?
No Tract in all this Isle, the proudest let her be,
Can shew a Sylvan Nymph, for beautie like to thee:
The Satyrs, and the Fawnes, by Dian set to keepe,
Rough Hilles, and Forrest holts, were sadly seene to weepe,
When thy high-palmed Harts the sport of Bowes and Hounds,
By gripple Borderers hands, were banished thy grounds.
The Driades that were wont about thy Lawnes to rove,
To trip from Wood to Wood, and scud from Grove to Grove,
On Sharpley that were seene, and Cadmans aged rocks,
Against the rising Sunne, to brayd their silver locks;
And with the harmlesse Elves, on Heathy Bardons height,
By Cynthia's colder beames to play them night by night,
Exil'd their sweet aboad, to poore bare Commons fled,
They with the Okes that liv'd, now with the Okes are dead.
Who will describe to life, a Forrest, let him take
Thy Surface to himselfe, nor shall he need to make
An other forme at all, where oft in thee is found
Fine sharpe but easie Hills, which reverently are crownd
With aged Antique Rocks, to which the Goats and Sheepe,
(To him that stands remoat) doe softly seeme to creepe,
To gnaw the little shrubs, on their steepe sides that grow;
Upon whose other part, on some descending Brow,
Huge stones are hanging out, as though they downe would drop,
Where under-growing Okes, on their old shoulders prop
The others hory heads, which still seeme to decline,
And in a Dimble neere, (even as a place divine,
For Contemplation fit) an Ivy-seeled Bower,
As Nature had therein ordayn'd some Sylvan power;
As men may very oft at great Assemblies see,
Where many of most choyce, and wondred Beauties be:
For Stature one doth seeme the best away to beare;
Another for her Shape, to stand beyond compare;
Another for the fine composure of a face:
Another short of these, yet for a modest grace
Before them all preferd; amongst the rest yet one,
Adjudg'd by all to bee, so perfect Paragon,

That all those parts in her together simply dwell,
For which the other doe so severally excell.
My Charnwood like the last, hath in her selfe alone,
What excellent can be in any Forrest showne.

1622   *Michael Drayton*

THE SHEPHERDESS

A shepherdess who long had kept her flocks
On stony Charnwood's dry and barren rocks,
In heat of summer to the vales declin'd
To seek fresh pasture for her lambs half pin'd;
She (while her charge was feeding) spent the hours
To gaze on sliding brooks, and smiling flowers.

17th C.   *Francis Beaumont*

ACROSS THE VALLEY

Blue are the swallow's darting wings,
And blue the dragon-fly;
Blue is the bloom on ripened grapes,
And blue the twilight sky;
Heavenly blue the crane's-bill flowers
That blow beside the lane;
But bluer than all are the Charnwood Hills,
Clear for the coming of rain.

1921   *Teresa Hooley*

ST MARY'S, WOODHOUSE

St. Mary-in-the-Elms, 1338,
Not in perpendicular, high soaring gothic,
Or anything ornate.
Lift the latch and enter;
Pause, pray and ponder
The mysteries of our human state.
The elms long gone, the holy place remains inviolate.

1992   *Robert Rankin*

SWITHLAND GREAT PIT

In Swithland now the water fills the pits,
water blackly dense from great depth
and cold as slate, even in high summer.
The dust and pollen gathers in stagnant swirls,
suspended in transparent tension, tight
with quivering insects on the brittle skin;
young oaks in leaf and the last of the bluebells vivid
where the rock shelves have gathered precarious grass.
The heat of the day bends the taut drumskin
of the flooded quarry in a vibration
which seems to roll across the sky's dark mirror.

John Ellis worked the Great Pit hard
for twenty-eight years, extracting massive slate
in fissured slabs, cleavages of exposed time.
The brown and faded photograph of him
shows him poised casually on the north edge
of the pit, where the deepest workings were,
a hundred and eighty feet of vertical drop.
There he is, looking ridiculous
in his rakish top hat and frock coat,
leaning against the beams of the wooden crane,
right hand in his pocket, legs crossed,
smugly lounging against the elemental
landscape he had created from the rock.

Leaving the cat curled in the alcove of the window
I turn at the top of the steps, pat the crown
of my hat, button my coat against the cold
of this September morning, and linger a while
as the heavy door behind me soundlessly closes,
like a sudden affair with a serving girl.
The village to my left is curtained in mist,
the parlours are empty and cold as the grey ash
flutters in the downdraughts of chimneys;
I assume servants light fires and stoves.

The smoke from my quarries clings low to the yellowing trees,
a reminder of one's living, like the death
of same-age friends. The knob of my cane is hard
in my hand, a welcome fact in the cup of my palm.
When I enter the quarry labourers touch their caps,
the craftsmen their black hats, call me sir.
The wet autumn slate dust is hanging
around our knees. At my age I can't always
miss the grey puddles in the soft ruts.
By the end of the day my legs are the colour of slate.

The last cart lurched down the cobbles of Leicester
loaded with Swithland slate in the stinging rain
of the hard winter of 1887.
It was Ellis's nightmare: terrace on terrace
of red-brick houses capped with uniform
and cheap Welsh slate, glistening black like coal.
He stood listening to the rain, to its hiss
as sharp as a chisel, to the cracking of traffic on stone
like the rip of silk as slate is split open.
The rock channels in the silent pits at home
filled with water even as he listened.

1992   *Steve Hobson*

VILLAGE FAIR ON ANSTEY GREEN

a week's pitch
in a green field
too small to support
a big wheel

glare, blare
and brightly
coloured canvas

lit up at
seven o-clock

children urgent
for sensation
swings and speed

next week

bruised grass
rutted gateways
as the small
creatures creep home

1992   *Berenice Moore*

from
BLACK ANNIS' BOWER

When down the plain the winding pathway falls
From Glenfield Vill to Lester's ancient walls,
Nature or Art with imitative power,
Far in the glen has placed Black Annis' Bower.

Here, if the uncouth song of former days
Soil not the page with Falsehood's artful lays,
Black Annis held her solitary reign,
The dread and wonder of the neighbouring plain.
The shepherd grieved to view his waning flock,
And traced his firstlings to the gloomy rock.
No vagrant children culled the flow'rets then,
For infant blood oft stained the gory den.

But Time, than Man more certain, tho' more slow,
At length 'gainst Annis drew his sable bow;
The great decree the pious shepherds bless'd,
And general joy the general fear confess'd.

18th C.   *John Heyrick*

from
PASSAGES AND ENTERTAINMENTS FROM LONDON TO LEICESTER

On Thursday, trotting, galloping and ambling,
To Leister, I proceeded in my rambling:
There, at the blue Boare I was welcome then
Unto my brother Miles, a downright man....
That house, King Richard lodg'd in, his last night,
Before he did the field of Bosworth fight,
And there's a Room, a King to entertain,
The like is not in Leister Town again,
Th'Assizes then were there, some causes tride,
And Law did there the corps and souls divide,
Of two offenders, one had with a Knife
Stabd his contracted love, and reav'd her life,
'Tother, a wench that had stolen some poor rayment,
And fir'd the house, deserv'd the Hangmans payment.
King Leir a Temple did to Janus reare
And plac'd a Flamine in't, there doth appeare
The arched Ovens foure yards thick at least,
Wherein they Heathen Sacrifices drest....
So people here, when warre or peace they fought;
They offrings unto Janus Temple brought;
This was eight hundred forty and foure yeare
Before our Saviours birth, built by King Leir,
Long after Eltredred (the Mercian King)
A happy and a Christian change did bring,
The Temple raz'd the Flamine he defac'd,
And there a Christian Bishops See he plac'd,
Which last but few yeares, for then this Land
Was seven-fold yoaked, beneath 7 Kings command,
And those Kings still were in perpetuall wars
That England was quite spoyl'd with endlesse jars,
And in those Garboyles Leister had her share,
Spoyl'd, rifled, ransack'd, rob'd, and left most bare,
Till Edelfred, with great magnificence,
Repair'd and wall'd it strongly for defence.
Then did it flourish long in wealth and state,
Till second Henry it did ruinate:
He in out-ragious fury fir'd the Town,
Diswall'd it quite, and cast the Castle down,
So nothing but some ruines doth appeare,
Whereby men may perceive that such things were.
Thus Leister fell, from state superlative,
Her fifty churches all consum'd to five.
Yet it is faire and spacious at this day,

36

And East, West, North and South 'tis every way
Above a mile in length, so that no doubt,
The Town's in circuit six large miles about.
Henry first Duke of Lancaster in war,
In peace, or bounty, a bright blazing Star
For buildings in this City is renown'd,
Which as time rais'd, time did again confound.
Yet one large fabrick there doth still abide,
Whereby the good Dukes name is dignifide.
And that's an Hospitall or Bead-house, where
One hundred and ten men are harbour'd there,
From perishing through want, still to defend
Those aged men untill the world shall end....
Good Henry Earle of Huntingdon (renown'd)
A free schoole did erect there, from the ground,
With means (though meane) for mayntenance endow'd
Two Ushers, and one Schoolmaster allow'd,
They teach young lads, such Rules as do belong,
To reade the English and the Latine tongue,
And when their knowledge is with hope discerned,
They in the Greek may learn, and be more learn'd.

1639   *John Taylor*

TO THE KING
Upon His Taking of Leicester

This Day is Yours, Great CHARLES! and in this War
Your Fate, and Ours, alike Victorious are.
In her white Stole, now Victory do's rest
Enspher'd with Palm on Your Triumphal Crest.
Fortune is now Your Captive; other Kings
Hold but her hand; You hold both hands and wings.

1648   *Robert Herrick*

DEATH OF WOLSEY
(Henry VIII, Act IV, Scene 2)

At last, with easy roads, he came to Leicester;
Lodg'd in the abbey, where the reverend abbot,
With all his convent, honourably receiv'd him:
To whom he gave these words: "O! father abbot,
An old man, broken with the storms of state,
Is come to lay his weary bones among ye;
Give him a little earth for charity."
So went to bed, where eagerly his sickness
Pursu'd him still; and three nights after this,
About the hour of eight, – which he himself
Foretold should be his last, – full of repentance.
Continual meditations, tears, and sorrows,
He gave his honours to the world again,
His blessed part to heaven, and slept in peace.

1623   *William Shakespeare*

THE RUINS AT BRADGATE

What wanton wreck is here, what sore decay!
What mournful tale these broken walls could tell
Of her, who, cast upon ambition's swell,
Must live in royal pomp her little day!
Made Queen in name, she sought no monarch's sway:
Its ninth day struck her reign's enforced knell,
Ended ere scarce begun; her head dissevered fell,
Sad trophy of her father's headstrong way.
Within these rooms she grew, in this retreat
In Plato's page she learned to study deep,
And walked with Cicero upon this mead:
Grass grows today on floors that felt her feet,
But still the torn house doth her memory keep,
While by its shattered porch the wild deer feed.

1950   *T.C. Hunter Clare*

from
THE WONDERFUL EFFECTS OF THE LEICESTER RAIL ROAD

Of all the great wonders that ever were known –
And some wonderful things have occurred in this town –
The Leicester rail road it will beat them all hollow;
And the man who first thought on't he was a fine fellow.

What a beautiful sight it is for to see
A long string of carriages on the railway,
All loaded with passengers, inside and out,
And moved by what comes from a tea-kettle's spout.

And then, what a lot of employment 'twill make,
The Leicester bricklayers may now undertake
To send ready-built houses to London by steam;
No doubt it will turn out a very good scheme.

Now any old woman that has enough sense
By raking and scraping to save eighteenpence,
In service in London if she has a daughter,
She may ride up and see her by this boiler of water.

And all coach proprietors who've rolled in wealth
Must ride upon donkeys for the good of their health,
And to keep up their spirits must strike up this theme
And curse all the rail roads and boiling hot steam.

c.1840   *Anon.*

PLACE RHYMES

Thorpe Arnold, four people,   Brentingby pancheons
Leather bells, wooden steeple.   And Wyfordby pans,
                                       Stapleford organs,
                                       And Burton tingtangs.

Hob, Shoby, and Grimston on the hill,
Wartnaby, Ab-Kettleby, and Little Ragdale.

Trad.

LEICESTER

Here on a wooded bank beside the River Leire
Mud huts house warriors hue dyed with woad,
But crude valour cannot stem the tramp of sandalled feet,
Nor halt the paving of a Roman road.

Here honest men can till the rich brown earth
And listen to the echo of the hunting horn,
As with the labour of stout hearts and yeoman hands
A gracious English county town is born.

Here many a staunch man of the Parliament
Strikes a fierce blow at Rupert's troop of horse,
And many an earnest stockinger with misplaced intent
Wrecks the hopes of the new frames by force.

Here works the hand maker of boots, shoes and hose,
To ply his trade with skill that all admires,
Until to-day, craftsmen, men and women in a mighty host,
Follow in the footsteps of their sturdy sires.

Here, that once was tangled thorn and quiet stream,
Stands true a city thronged with industry and fame,
Whose tides of commerce flood the four corners of the earth
With symbols of a proud and honoured name.

1949   *G.H. Ingles*

from
SAXON LADY

By Leicester's Jewry Wall
Near Saxon pots,
The Roman painted walls,
Flints, bronze and medieval bric-a-brac
She lies alone.
Forever still inside her case of glass
Coffined to wait upon
The trumpet call to Resurrection
Through long elements of time.
Brown skull, brown bones
With bangle, torque and ring
To hold for ever; hers.
She lies alone, prepared perhaps
For silent hours each night
The City quiets itself.
This Saxon lady sleeps.
She died, the notice says
Sometime before the year
Six hundred Anno Domini.
It tells no more.
She rests away slow measured days
And is my distant kin
Or cousin, far removed.
Who, for a while was host
To specks of DNA, the genes,
Passed, running through
Our busy English relay race
To me.

1988   *Peter Godfrey*

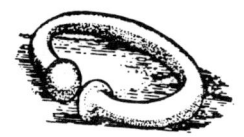

WHAT YO'VE NEVER

What yo've never yakked stale bread hard on
To them swans and ducks, when no one looked on
Abbey Park. Stood and shouted for the Tigers on
Boxing Day feeling slightly sick. Had two cream cakes on
Top of ice cream sodas at that cafe just because on
the next day after seeing Daniel Lambert you were on
                    a very strick diet.

What yo've never had chips on
Vicky Park, ate your cheese cobs on
Town Hall square, watched the lovers dodge pigeons on
A Wednesday market, bought too much fruit cause it was cheap on
That stall with the man that sure could spin a yarn on
Thursday seen the fruit cheaper at the local shop.

What yo've never laid on bracken and deer droppings on
Bradgate Park, ate stale Melton Mowbray pie on
That hard seat near Lady Jane Grey's on
A wet Sunday afternoon with the dog on
The same day the lad's kite got stuck on
Old John, and after that can of pop there were no-where to pee on.
What yo've never, oh! yo've never lived in Leicester long.

1990   *Sarah Wallace*

RAP GUIDE TO LEICESTER

Daniel Lambert, William Wyggeston,
Thomas Cook, Alderman Newton.

Bradgate, Beacon, Jewry Wall,
Haymarket Theatre, De Montfort Hall.

Richard the Third, Lady Jane Grey,
Bosworth Field, The Old Fosse Way.

Tigers, Foxes, we've got them all,
So come to Leicester for a bit of a ball!

1992   *Debbie Beck*

MEMORIES OF LEICESTER

The lovely old trams that rattled along,
From Horsefair Street or Humberstone.
The Town Hall Square, the fountain's spray,
The Theatre Royal to watch a play.
The market, open till nine o'clock,
"Ere y'are, gimme a tanner for this lot, me duck."
St Margaret's pastures, Abbey Park lake
(Where Leicester spent its holiday break).
The news revolving round Thomas Cook's,
The Japanese Gardens at Aylestone Cut;
Bedfordshire Clangers*, no thought to slim,
New corn flakes called "Sunny Jim".
Jack Sills' boots to fit any foot,
The Star Picture House in the tup'ny rush.
"Charny"*...... Ah...... The great display,
From a safety pin to a brewer's dray.
The "Sallies"* with the big brass band,
Marched round the Tower...... ooh, it wer grand!
Forgive us if we brush a tear,
For the memories of Leicester we hold so dear.

1992   *Bel Weldon*

* Bedfordshire Clanger: Large suet pudding, filled with meat and onions and boiled forever in a cloth.
* Charny: Charnwood Street, a very old shopping area in Leicester much loved by the natives and visitors alike, now sadly demolished after extensive bombing in 1940.
* Sallies: The Salvation Army who marched through the town every Sunday evening and round the Clock Tower.

ST NICHOLAS CHURCH, LEICESTER
10.1.1980 (In memory of G. S. Fraser, poet, tutor)

I feel at home here,
It's friendly, welcoming;
The gentle arch accessible,
Apt as a metaphor.

Sun warms stone walls,
Irregular blocks
Stained ochre by iron,
Bricks of a farmhouse kitchen.

We are square-set,
No narrow elongation,
Rather
A seminar.

Outside, light sparks on a diamond pane
A jubilation.
It dims; this is winter,
A funeral service. Warmth has gone.

1986   *Emma Gleadall*

STONEYGATE AFTERNOON

L   eafy sun-dappled sentinels line London Road, Stoneygate.
E   legant Victorian architecture, preserved for posterity, stands
I   ll at ease with its contemporary counterparts.
C   hattering children, disgorged from discreet private schools,
E   rupt onto previously pristine pavements.
S   ocially mobile matrons wend their way "Bridgewards"
T   ongues tripping on scandalous topical titbits.
E   xhausted au pairs, dreaming of "apres tea",
R   ound up reluctant charges and hurry home to freedom.

1992   *Doris Paul-Clark*

THE ROOKERIES, AYLESTONE

Fair spot; where I have often found delight,
And sought your shade by morning and by night;
There I have watched the Sunset, glorious scene!
And the queen Moon arise with light serene,
The flowers and birds did ever welcome give,
Teaching the minstrel how to nobly live;
And when the stars were shining from on high
Your trees peered forth in silent majesty.
When the glad Sun, from o'er the Eastern hills,
The Soar's sweet valley with his brightest fills,
Strong sons of labour to the fields repair,
For future harvests they the soil prepare;
With song and laughter they their toil relieve,
Industrious workers have not time to grieve.
And as I sit and meditate on men,
These various scenes give ardour to my pen.
I dream of mornings in the bygone years,
When sorrowing mourners passed these trees in tears,
As from Glen's village they their loved ones bore
To bury in "God's acre" by the Soar.
A sacred spot to them was Ayleston's shrine,
Which they would visit and on graves recline,
And mourn for those white spirits of the just.
The place is sacred, and whate'er befall,
This is my Altar, my great Banquet Hall.
And thus I muse in evening's sacred hour
Midst hum of bee and fragrance of the flower.
The Sun is setting, still I wander here,
The Rookeries my mind and spirit cheer.

1902   *John Dainty*

PLACE RHYMES

Mountsorrel is a stony place,   Markfield on the hill,
Pretty Quorn is sandy,   Newtown in the vale,
Sileby is the devil's hole   Groby for silly beggars,
And Barrow is the dandy.   And Ratby for ale.

When mist doth rise from Belvoir Hole,
O, thou be sure the weather's foul.

Trad.

45

MEMORIES OF THE GRAND UNION

When I was a kid
I'd walk down to the Cut
With a bag full of bits
To feed the ducks.
Me mam stood beside me
As I meted out bread,
And the stories she told me
Still run through my head.
'Bout how the Grand Union
Was built for the boats,
And coal barges so heavy,
'Twas a wonder they'd float.
And the old shire horses
Would pull them along,
Treading the towpaths
All mighty and strong –
'Bout the navvies who built it
With blood, sweat and tears.
How long did it take 'em?
How many years?
1992

And as she told me
It seemed in my head
I could see them and smell them
And hear what they said
An' as I'd stood dreamin'
My mam'd whisper to me –
"Stop your wool gatherin,
It's time fer yer tea."
I'd look around startled,
Surprised only to see
Just the ducks on the water,
Me mother an' me.
So homeward we'd traipse
With a last look behind
At the murky deep waters,
Left to remind
Of the uses to which these
Canals were once put.
Yes, I savour the hours
Spent down by the Cut.

Linda Mary Hudson

46

DOWN MEMORY LANE

Down memory lane, where are we going now?
To Walton, where I knew
A mulberry bush grew
With red fruit and leafy green bough;
The little chapel where children sang
"Joyful, joyful will the meeting be,
When from sin our hearts are pure and free";
And Sunday School Treats, with lots of eats
At Wickstead, where the lake seemed like the sea.

At South Wigston level crossing,
As steam trains thundered past,
We were there to wave, as the driver gave
A long, long whistle blast
And so as we lay in our beds,
We heard the noise from Wigston sheds –
The bing, bang, bong of buffers meeting
And the shunters' shouted greeting.

Then in winter's ice and snow
The coal trains started, Oh so slow,
And as the drive wheels skidded round
The smoke stack made a rapid chuffing sound.
Down Crow Mills it was tiddlers in
With cane rod, cotton and bent pin;
It was sticklebacks and stony roach we were after,
Pulled out to the sound of laughter.

Down memory lane, where are you taking me now?
As the wrinkles deepen on my brow
It's good to remember things long past,
So here's to memories, long may they last.

1992   *Harry Slaney*

OADBY TOWN

Elegant shops – smart, fresh and clean –
Still retain the village scene.
Spoilt for choice to feast the eyes;
Health foods, cheeses, large pork pies.
"Oh, look, dear, what a lovely sweet",
(Seems to have gone a bit deaf this week).

Just one street, and all of this,
(The feet are grateful, oh what bliss!).
"Where is this place?" you ask and frown,
So glad you asked because it's... Oadby Town.

1992   *Bel Weldon*

EASTER SUNDAY, BURROUGH HILL

I climbed with morning, waking only crows,
And watched the sunrise from the Iron Age fort,
An upturned pudding basin wrapped in green;
From where, they say, a keen-eyed man can see
Three counties, when the sun burns off the mist.
I ate, but did not roll, the hard-boiled eggs,
And walked back through the cattle studded fields
Still sleeping under cold grey sheets of dew.

I passed, beneath some trees, an old ram skull,
Bleached white and nailed to a rotting post;
A grinning relic of more pagan days
With nightshade garlands twined about its horns.

I let myself into the silent house,
And washed, and brought you tea and toast in bed.

1992   *Dylan Pugh*

THE REAL MELTON MOWBRAY

What can be said about Melton Mowbray?
That fox-hunting gave her that world-wide renown?
That curds become Stilton; that curdless whey
Fattens the porkers for pies raised in town?
That pubs like the Mash Tub, Wheatsheaf, and Crown,
And churches and chapels, lodges and halls,
And an old Court House where Justices frown,
Are *it*, (with twice-a-week Street Market stalls)?
No! Melton is people paying back calls
To neighbours and friends who live in their street,
Tending the lonely, raising him who falls,
And helping the sad troubled souls they meet,
Because they're made that way – their hearts are kind:
They are the *real* Melton – or so I find!

1992   *Dan Pugh*

THE RAIN
(Melton Mowbray)

The rain burning down over Nottingham Road
Illuminates the sky like stars in the midst of night,
A slow reflection of the past everywhere,
The blocks of flats and housing estates
Where the fields used to spread out into the distance,
The entanglement of road where once the playground echoed with laughter.

We look out and everything is different,
Even the air and the clouds and the landscape.
The memories remain constant like dreams,
Never fading until the spirit has died.

1992   *Shaun Johnson*

49

BELVOIR CASTLE
Inscription in the Duchess's Garden

One cultivated spot behold, which spreads
Its flowery bosom to the noontide beam –
Where num'rous rosebuds rear their blushing heads,
And poppies rich, and fragrant violets teem.
Far from the busy world's unceasing sound –
Here has Eliza fixed her favourite seat,
Chaste emblem of the scene around –
Pure as the flower that smiles beneath her feet.

Early 19th C.   *John Henry Manners,*
                    5th Duke of Rutland

ON LEAVING BELVOIR CASTLE
Lines written in 1842

Farewell, fair castle! on thy lordly hill
Firm be thy seat and proud thy station still,
Soft rise the breezes from the vale below,
Bright be the clouds that wander o'er thy brow;
O'er the broad lands that form thy wide domain
Short be the winter, long the summer's reign.
Pilgrim of pleasure to thy stately towers,
Fain would I leave among thy friendly bowers
Some votive offering ere on my way,
With many a backward glance, I turn to stray.
May virtue, strength, and honour, guard thy walls,
Love, health, and peace, abide within thy halls,
While graceful mirth and noble courtesy
As now for ever hold their seat in thee;
And still upon thy lordly turrets rest
The grateful blessing of each parting guest!

1883   *Frances Anne Kemble*

BELVOIR BATTLE

Sour milk becomes Stilton and curdleas whey –
And north of Melton, behind hedge and rail,
Sleek black-and-white cows eating away
The rich green pastures of fair Belvoir Vale.

Almost on top of the Jubilee trail
Tall drilling-rigs bore for coal, gas and oil,
Making the faces of residents pale,
Lest coal-mining their environment spoil.

Conservationists in horror recoil
When pro-mining parties advocate haste;
And grazing cows keep manuring rich soil
That soon may be lost beneath heaps of waste.

But Belvoir Castle broods over the whole,
As arguments rage – for farming? Or coal?

1992   *Dan Pugh*

from
LYINGHAM*

This dismal village stands in Bumpkinshire*
That fertile county farmers all admire,
Where bullocks, sheep and hogs do much abound,
With yet more hoggish tillers of the ground;
Where freely, too, the cunning foxes rove,
And feed the joyous sport that hunters love.
The straggling village and its clownish band,
Its dingy houses crumbling as they stand,
Its mud-built walls, its dirty, ill-kept green,
Where sorry curs and squalling brats are seen,
Its vulgar roisterers in their foolish glee,
Its hideous hags so ready for a fee,
Its easy maids who know not virtue's name,
And hold of little worth their virgin fame;
No forms of tedious courtship they require,
But ripely yield to each expressed desire;

*

Nor can the village boast of Nature's charms,
Although it lies 'mid large and fertile farms.
Around it rise no purple tinted hills,
Nor through its fields meander sparkling rills;
The dreary calm that broods o'er all around
Is never broken by a pleasant sound;
No gladsome birds e'er sing at eve or morn;
No fragrant flowers the cottage plots adorn;
No odours sweet are waft on summer breeze;
No pleasant shadows fall from stately trees;
No saints, but many sinners in it dwell;
And strangers brand it still with curses fell;
For from fair July till leafy June
There is always some foolery full in tune;
And altogether 'tis a wretched spot
Where no sane man would wish to cast his lot.

1879   *?John Elkington*

*Lyingham = Wymondham
*Bumpkinshire = Leicestershire

RUTLAND

MULTUM·IN·PARVO

RUTLAND

Return to us our stone-built Rutland,
Seventeen down, the same across;
For now we stand knee-deep on upland
Barley'd wold and mourn our loss.
Surrender every golden summer,
Every sleepy afternoon;
Despatch this instant news with runner,
All will be delivered soon.

Return to us our ancient churches,
Fifty, and no two alike;
Taken, not by legal purchase –
Counties shuffled in the night.
Yield the quarries stony heartland
Rocks from Rutland's gaping wounds;
Pluck it from its new found outland,
Tell us it will happen soon.

Relinquish all your rights to Rutland;
Uppingham and Oakham towns,
Have Mercia on ancient upland,
Royal forests, sunlit downs;
Pastoral East Midland valleys,
Snickets, avenues and lanes;
Plundered now our roads and alleys,
Once defended from the Danes.

1988   *Mike Read*

SMALL SHIRE
(Poly-Olbion, Song XXIV)

Love not thy selfe the lesse, although the least thou art,
What thou in greatnesse wantst, wise Nature doth impart
In goodnesse of thy soyle; and more delicious mould,
Survaying all this Isle, the Sunne did nere behold.
Bring forth that British Vale, and be it ne'r so rare,
But Catmus with that Vale, for richnesse shall compare:
What Forrest-Nymph is found, how brave so ere she be,
But Lyfield shewes her selfe as brave a Nymph as shee?
What River ever rose from Banke, or swelling Hill,
Then Rutlands wandring Wash, a delicater Rill?
Small Shire that can produce to thy proportion good,
One Vale of speciall Name, one Forrest, and one Flood.
O Catmus, thou faire Vale, come on in Grasse and Corne,
That Bever ne'r be sayd thy sister-hood to scorne,
And let thy Ocham boast, to have no little grace,
That her the pleased Fates, did in they bosome place,
And Lyfield, as thou art a Forrest, live so free,
That every Forrest-Nymph may praise the sports in thee.
And downe to Wellands course, O Wash, runne ever cleere,
To honour, and to be much honoured by this Shire.

1622   *Michael Drayton*

MELTON TO OAKHAM CANAL*

There alongside swingbridge gate
Long boats on the canal do wait;
Pulled into locks on long haul ropes,
Boatmen chanting songs of hope,
Horses straining against the load –
Household goods, textiles and soap.
Melton to Oakham is their goal,
Grain for the mill, wool and coal.

1992   *Peter Morriss*

*Oakham Canal is now disused. Only parts remain, used for fishing.

RUTLAND
(from The Counties of England)

Here it was always a summer evening. An obsolete
Male population of steeplejacks trail, through the Uppingham streets
And the alleys of Oakham, traditional portions of woodsmoke
Homewards to wives in their cottages dreaming as ever of cheeses:
While over the toby-jug factory, over the orchard of cherries
Creeps the abolishing shadow of wicked Squire Locust of Gall.

1986   *John Bull*

MY LORD OF BUCKINGHAM'S WELCOME TO THE KING AT BURLEY

Sir, you have ever shin'd upon me bright,
But now, you strike and dazzle me with light:
You England's radiant sun, vouchsafe to grace
My house, a sphere too little and too base;
My Burley as a cabinet contains
The gem of Europe, which from golden veins
Of glorious princes, to this height is grown,
And joins their precious virtues all is one:
My thoughts with zeal, and earnest fervour press
Which should be first, and their officious strife
Restrains my hand from painting you to life.
I write, and having written, I destroy,
Because my lines have bounds, but not my joy.

1629   *Sir John Beaumont*

EGLETON

I've explored the tiny county, but I'll not have had my fill
Till I've had a look at Egleton, near Burley on the Hill.

Anon.

THE OAKHAM POACHERS

Young men in every station
That live within this nation,
Pray hear my lamentation,
A solemn awful tale.
Concerning three young men
That now do lie condemned,
And heavy bound in irons
In Oakham county gaol.

On the ninth of January,
Against the law contrary,
Five young men unwary,
A poaching went we here.
Epping old wood did ramble
And fired at pheasants random
Among the bushes and brambles,
Which brought the keeper near.

The keepers did not venture,
Nor care the woods to enter,
But outside near the centre
In ambush there they stood.
The poachers being tired,
As to fly away required,
At length young Perkins fired,
He spilt the keeper's blood.

He on the ground lay crying,
But no assistance nigh him,
Like one that was a dying,
His blood in streams did flow.
Our way for home were making
With nine pheasants we had taken,
Another keeper faced us,
We fired at him also.

Then we were taken with speed,
For this inhuman deed,
Which caused our hearts to bleed
When we were to prison sent.
The assizes they were near,
And one of our comrades swore
That we three brothers fired,
For it we do not repent.

Their names I now will mention,
John, Robert, and George Perkins,
Three brothers tried for poaching,
Found guilty as we hear.
Unto the judge they cried,
Pray mercy don't deny us,
Oh! do my lord have mercy,
Upon our tender years.

May he who feeds the raven
Grant them peace from heaven,
May their sins be forgiven,
Ere they resign their breath.
There ne'er were three brothers
Before condemned together
Within a dreary prison
And sentenced unto death.

So all young men take warning,
And don't the law be scorning,
For in our days just dawning
We are cut off in our prime.
So don't the laws be scorning,
Two of them are transported,
The other hung at Oakham,
May God forgive their crime.

Late 1840s   *Anon.*

BARLEY

In Rutland, old Rutland, as I can recall,
The village of Barley is the best place of all.
The girls of old Barley are the plagues of our lives,
But when they are married they make excellent wives.

Anon.

OF EXTON'S TOP STREET

To those of fertile and romantic mind,
This ancient street is quite a find,
Its cottages of weathered stone
Some terraced – some stand quite alone.
The sun breaks through aft' morning rain,
The reeded thatch slopes clear of window frames,
And puddles now reflect their diamond panes,
Which glint and throw a thousand shafts of light,
Drawing the eye to such a heartening sight,
For here no traffic loud disturbs the calm,
No other sound but chickens on the lawn,
Stirred to activity, with coming of the dawn.
Now to less mundane thoughts, we bend our minds,
As distantly horizon finds....
No end to Top Street's charming lines,
Let solitude our companion be
As village fades quite suddenly
To form backcloth to field and tree,
No longer buildings there to see,
Nor signs of domesticity,
The birds above trill endlessly
Small creatures scurry in the lee
Of sheltering hedge, or mature tree,
A pleasing portraiture, I find,
To elevate both heart and mind!

1992   *Robert Woolfe Tims*

from
IN THE RUINS OF PICKWORTH, RUTLAND
Elegy Hastily Composed & Written with a Pencil on the spot

These buried Ruins now in dust forgot
These heaps of stone the only remnants seen
The "Old Foundations" still they call the spot
Which plainly tells Enquiry what has been

A time was once – tho' now the nettle grows
In triumph o'er each heap that swells the ground
When they in buildings pil'd a village rose
With here a Cot and there a Garden crownd

And here while Grandeur with unequal share
Perhaps maintained its idleness and pride
Industry's cottage rose contented there
With scarce as much as wants of life supplied

*

Ye scenes of desolation spread around
Prosperity to you did once belong
And doubtless where these brambles claim the ground
The glass once flow'd to hail the ranting song

The alehouse here might stand – each hamlet's boast
And here where elders rich from ruin grows
The tempting sign – but what was once is lost
Who would be proud of what this world bestows?

How contemplation mourns your lost decay
To view thy pride laid level with the ground
To see where labour clears the soil away
What fragments of mortality abound.

1822   *John Clare*

LINES ON WISHING WELL AT ASHWELL

All ye who hither come to drink
Rest not your thoughts below
Look at that sacred sign and think
Whence living waters flow.

                              Anon.

59

EMPINGHAM

High o'er the rivulet
Stands the grey edifice,
Middle Age artifice,
Guarding the village.

Grave stones are lichenous,
Frailty is evident,
Human life transient,
God is abiding.

Spires speak with eloquence:
Faith has transcendency,
Hope has ascendancy,
Love is abiding.

Arabis, daffodils,
As you come travelling
Over the gravelling,
Wayfarers welcome.

White horse of Hanover
Prances amazingly
On royal blazonry
Over the north door.

Slabs from sarcophagi
Speak of feudality
And of mortality
Even of magnates.

From the spent centuries
Issues a history
Hid half in mystery,
Shrouded in questions.

Who are the characters
Scarcely now visible,
Hardly perceptible,
Faded on plaster?
1992

Solemn antiquary
Seeks for sedilia,
Memorabilia,
Pondering Pevsner.

Aumbries so plentiful,
Arms of de Normanville,
Traces of Mackworth will
Fill him with pleasure.

Summertime visitor,
Clad in the casual,
Seeking the usual,
Has his delight too.

Feeling no urgency,
Ambling so leisurely,
Half unexpectedly
Glimpses the angels.

Splendid and durable,
Stouter than masonry,
Subtler than tracery,
Grace is abounding.

Here there is holiness,
Here's no museum sight
Nor mausoleum night.
Worship is valid.

Kneeling in prayerfulness
Touch the intangible,
View the invisible
God ever constant.

J. E. Swaby

GREAT CASTERTON
Written in April at Walk Lodge

Long sweeping bends of croppings brightning green
That wind along the vallies sheltering crown
Large swelling hills that nauntle up the scene
Which winter pencil tips wi' bleachy brown
Here steeple points and there a misty town
As stretching thro' each opening to be seen
And woods enlivning from their gloomy hue
To sprout in freshness – while the heath hills lean
In triumph on the eye their blooming goss
Wild nature's brightest ornaments as now
Speckt o'er wi' sheep and beast and nibbling horse
That still roamd free from the long lazy plough
And the horizon sweeping faintly blue
That prickt its bordering circle round the view.

1821   *John Clare*

GREAT CASTERTON

Think now this glancing sunlight falls
Along the dreaming roofs of farms and cottages
And over the great white road
Whipping down out of the summer air
Quick like a shooting star
Under the canopies of branches
To the top of the distant hill,
How once the poet Clare
Walked sick at heart these daisied meadowlands.
Speech broke from him like a sweat
When he, dumb villager, saw thrushes' nests
Alive with smooth new eggs,
And quiet streams, and swishing cows,
This same grey church, the little inn
A maze of smoke and country talk,
And heard across the milkwhite coppices
The birds of Rutland sing
And all the bells crash out from Ryhall and from Empingham.

1953   *Leonard Clark*

NORMANTON
(The Fleece, Book I)

On spacious airy downs and gentle hills,
With grass and thyme o'erspread, and clover wild,
Where smiling Phoebus tempers every breeze,
The fairest flocks rejoice: they, nor of halt,
Hydropic tumours, nor of rot, complain,
Evils deform'd and foul; nor with hoarse cough
Disturb the music of the pastoral pipe;
But, crowding to the note, with silence soft
The close-woven carpet graze, where Nature blends
Flowerets and herbage of minutest size,
Innoxious luxury. Wide airy downs
Are Health's gay walks to shepherd and to sheep.

All arid soils, with sand or chalky flint,
Or shells deluvian mingled, and the turf
That mantles over rocks of brittle stone,
Be thy regard; and where low-tufted broom,
Or box, or berried juniper, arise;   .
Or the tall growth of glossy-rinded beech;
And where the burrowing rabbit turns the dust;
And where the dappled deer delights to bound.

*

... such the clover'd lawns
And sunny mounts of beauteous Normanton,
Health's cheerful haunt, and the selected walk
Of Heathcote's leisure.

1757   *John Dyer*

THE TRAVELLER'S RETURN

"In my dreams I e'er did long", said the traveller
                        by Rutland Water,
"To see the playful breeze make fun of the sails
                        on Rutland Water.

To see the rolling fields once more, the fishermen's
                        far off gaze,
As they scan the white clouds scudding by, thro' the
                        early morning haze.

So now in the autumn of my life", said the traveller
                        by Rutland Water,
"My wand'ring's done, and I have come back home
                        to Rutland Water."

1992   *Bel Weldon*

SUDDENLY, FROM THE PURPLE
(Welland Viaduct)

A slow, down goods
Rumbles on the viaduct,
Checked by amber.
Today is under no pressure to hurry,
A school-bound boy dawdle day,
Idle as summer scent
Sent out by roses
To entice,
Setting in motion the noses
Of half asleep mice;

Between bricks the dusty spider
Waits unimpatiently
To take forfeit in blood
The fly's outrage
Of the ruptured thread;

In the field a mare snoozes.
A dog rose loses
A petal to the breeze
At a bee's nudge.

Suddenly, from the purple
(Woody nightshade petal purple)
Sky, hammered down like thunder
From the ash tree under
The arch of blue brick,
A carrion crow
Bodily,
Like a ripped branch
Brokenly;

Crashing into the grass
It struck a spark,
Forced out a blackbird screaming,
Stabbed once
Then rose,
A chick in its beak,
Anticipating,
Back to the ash.

1992   *Philip Ennis*

SONNET ON THE RIVER GASH

Where winding Gash wirls round its wildest scene
On this romantic bend I sit me down
On that side view the meads their smoothing green
Edg'd with the peeping hamlets checkering brown
Here the steep hill as dripping headlong down
While glides the stream a silver streak between
As glides the shaded clouds along the sky
Brightning and deep'ning loosing as they're seen
In light and shade – so when old willows lean
Thus their broad shadow – runs the river bye
With tree and bush repleat a wilderd scene
And mossd and ivyd sparkling on my eye –
O thus wild musing am I doubly blest
My woes unheeding – and my heart at rest.

1820   *John Clare*

FOOTPATH TO LYDDINGTON

Lyddington, one and three-quarters;
The County counted miles have no regard
For gradient. On the ridge
A feral plot suggests sinister recollection
Of a previous occupation. Bramble and rampant
Rosebay willowherb rejoice in redundancy
Of the small concrete shelter – or perhaps
Presage ultimate fires.
Another ridge above warrened hawthorn and kek
Sparkles with daisies where the cold college
Rides a medieval swell, surging to
A lost lane, high-sided with oak
Ash and elder. From deep, damp green
Celandine and ladies smock reflect,
Through the blackbirds' panicky clatter,
Silent, invisible stars.

1958   *Barry Roberts*

PLACE RHYMES

Lines on the Gate Inn, Sibson

This gate hangs well
And hinders none
Refresh and pay
And travel on.

When Bardon Hill has a cap,
Hay and grass will suffer for that.

Whitwick

Nought remains of Talbot's name
But Talbot Wood and Talbot Lane.

Stretton in the Street,
Where shrews meet.

Trad.

BELTON IN RUTLAND

Have you sat on Lambley Hill
When the church bells ring?
Have you walked on Loddo Road
And seen the ironstone spring?
Have you strolled down Oakham Hill
To hear the yaffle cry?
Have you crept down Norgat Hedge
And watched the fox slink by?

We moved here many years ago
To escape the life in town.
We've levelled the potato patch
And laid a new lawn down.
At the bottom of the garden
We've dug a pond with pump.
And all around a conifer hedge
Over which the dog can't jump.

We haven't been to Lambley;
The hill is much too far.
We haven't walked on Loddo;
But we've passed there in the car.
And Oakham Hill is steep;
Just grass verges and the trees.
And Norgat Hedge has potholes
With mud up to your knees.

1992   *Anon.*

THE ANCIENT ONE
(Braunston)

Here I stand as the years go by,
Made in stone,
But not of human hand.
An ancient god of forgotten times.
I watch man as he passes by;
Once he danced for me,
Now looks on with puzzled awe.
Defaced,
And once used as a step into the church,
Many Christian footsteps have trodden me down,
But being of stone,
My soul it does not hurt.
Legend says I move around,
One day by the tower wall,
Next, I'm not there at all.
Now upright again, I proudly stand.
So come,
And let our spirits unite.
Once again dance with me,
With garlanded hair,
From past unto future,
Into this ancient land.

1992   *J.R. Naylor*

NOW ROBIN LEND TO ME THY BOW
(Uppingham)

Now Robin lend to me thy bow,
Sweet Robin lend to me thy bow,
For I must now a-hunting with my Lady go,
With my sweet Lady go.

And whither will thy Lady go?
Sweet Wilkin tell it unto me:
And thou shalt have my hawk, my hound, and eke my bow
To wait on thy Lady.

My Lady will to Uppingham,
To Uppingham forsooth will she,
And I myself appointed for to be the man
To wait on my Lady.

Adew good Wilkin all beshrewd,
Thy hunting nothing pleaseth me,
But yet beware thy babbling hounds stray not abroad,
For angring of thy Lady.

My hounds shall be led in the line,
So well I can assure it thee:
Unless by view of strain some pursue I may find,
To please my sweet Lady.

With that the Lady she came in,
And will'd them all for to agree.
For honest hunting never was accounted sin,
Nor never shall for me.

1609   *Anon.*

69

ECHOES OF UPPINGHAM

Ring out old Bells of Uppingham,
Ring out, ring out,
How have you caught the life, the glow
Of hearts, and boyhood's eddying flow,
To clash it forth,
With music and a shout,
In tumbling waves of sound,
All down and round.

Ring out old Bells of Uppingham,
Go forth, old Bells,
O'er ancient School and gables grey,
Through wreathed nooks and flowery spray;
Each flower, each wreath,
A young boy's hope – ah, well –
Each lichen clinging there,
Old memories fair.

Ring out old Bells of Uppingham,
In changeful swells.
Ring, freighted full with smiles and tears,
The hoard of thrice a hundred years,
All boyhood's heart,
Jests, sorrows, hopes, and knells,
With Taylor's holy lore
Sweet as of yore.

Ring out old Bells of Uppingham,
Roll down the vale,
'Twixt these low hills, o'er pleasant grass,
Round feeding sheep, by ash trees pass,
Pass down the vale,
Steal with the Welland on
By hamlet, tower, and lea,
Lost in the sea.

Ring out old Bells of Uppingham,
We'll go with you,
A breathing charm o'er dale and hill,
A voice for every good and ill,
To brethren true,
From some old church at last
A voice still rolling on,
When we are gone.

1856   *Edward Thring*

INDEX OF POETS